Out Of This Box

Poems and Reflections on Being Human

by Sandy Amodio

Copyright 2011, Sandy Amodio

All rights reserved. No part of this book may be reproduced without written permission from the publisher, except for brief passages for review purposes.

Contact Information: sandyamodio@gmail.com

Illustration websites (public domain):

http:// www.oldbookillustrations.com,

http://www.reusableart.com, http://wwwclker.com

http:// www.freevintageimages.com,

http:// fithfath.com

Illustration on page 125: linocut by Jack Baumgartner

Cover photo: Tim Serneels

Printed in Canada

You desire to know the art of living, my friend? It is contained in one phrase: make use of suffering. ~ Henri-Frederic Amiel

Be glad of life because it gives you the chance to love and to work and to play and to look up at the stars. ~Henry Van Dyke

There are very few human beings who receive the truth, complete and staggering, by instant illumination. Most of them acquire it fragment by fragment, on a small scale, by successive developments, like a laborious mosaic. ~Anaïs Nin

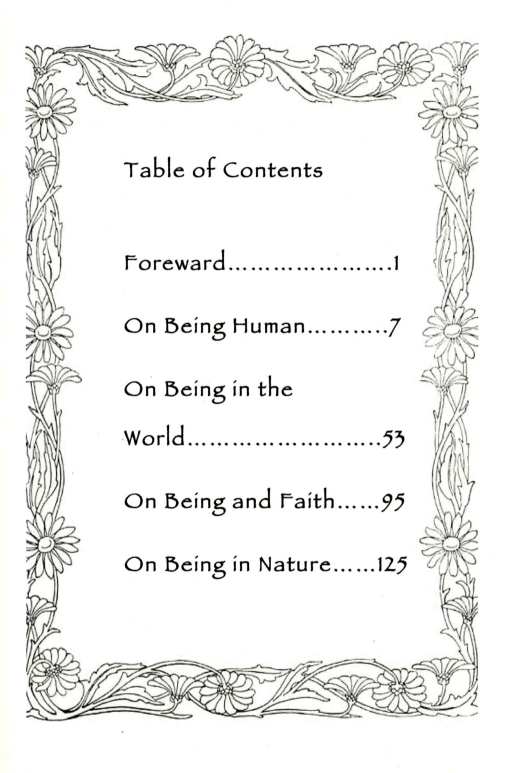

Table of Contents

Foreward........................1

On Being Human..........7

On Being in the World.........................53

On Being and Faith......95

On Being in Nature......125

Foreward

FOR SEVERAL YEARS I struggled to write a novel, because it is the most popular and marketable thing to produce as an author. Try as I might, I couldn't get past the first few chapters. I started out with great intent and enthusiasm, but quickly ran out of steam. I didn't want to accept that perhaps I wasn't meant to be a novelist. By contrast, poetry came much more naturally, and when I surrendered to this truth, I began to forget about what was more popular and enjoy myself. Though at times I am still reluctant to say that I am a poet, because it calls up images of corny greeting cards, I am content with this humble, yet profound pursuit, and to forget about what others might think.

Poetry has always been a lifeline for me, especially being an introvert who felt quite anxious in social situations. When I went through hard times, there were a handful of poems I would turn to, reading and reciting them as often as I needed to. Mary Oliver's *Wild Geese* was one of my favorites. When I was a little girl, about ten, I used to sit at the desk in my room and write poems, or copy them out of books, enough handwritten copies to deliver one page to each house on our street, about thirty homes in total. I would roll them up into scrolls, tie them with ribbons and run quickly to each house and drop them in the mailbox. I'm not sure what the purpose was-perhaps just to share something that was meaningful to me, or maybe I hoped the words in the poems might cheer someone up.

When I was sixteen I took a job as a summer camp counselor with the Salvation Army, a camp for underprivileged children from housing projects in the poorest parts of the city. In the evenings before my campers went to bed, we would gather in a circle on the wood floor, and I would read poetry from a collection that my mother gave me- a large, silver book called *Lines to Live By*. One by one the girls would call out a page number, and I would read a poem from that page. They listened intently, cross-legged in their flannel nightgowns and pajamas, with sunburned, earnest faces and tangled hair. Some of them had never heard poetry read aloud before. Many of them lived in homes where the language used was mostly cursing! They enjoyed the rhythms, the words, the images, and kept asking for more. I enjoyed reading as much as they loved to listen. It was a magical time in that circle of eager ten- year old girls, and sometimes I wish I could be transported back to that time, even just for an evening. Though poetry, like some other skills and crafts, has gone by the wayside, it still offers the gift of capturing some moment, idea, feeling, or image that can be shared with others. A poem can be something to hold on to, that makes us feel less alone and vulnerable. Poems can make us laugh, cry, wonder, and even make changes in our lives. There are famous people in the world, such as Nelson Mandela, who managed to survive terrible ordeals partly because of a poem that inspired them or kept them going each day. The world master's rowing champion, Sara Hall, often referred to Mary Oliver's poem called *The Journey* when she needed inspiration to keep focused on her love of rowing during a difficult marriage. Poems, unlike novels, are short enough that one can remember them for a long time.

Reading and writing poetry teaches us to be more observant of the world around us. This mindfulness seems to be increasingly absent from our lives as we become more focused on technology. Many people spend more time looking at computer screens or hunched over their text messages than observing the intricacies and wonders of the world around them.

Because many poems are written from true experiences and important insights, they connect us to others and their view of the world at a certain point in time. Some of my favorite poems are those written by soldiers in the world wars, who needed to express the deep sorrow and unforgettable pain of their war experiences. When I read them I can imagine these soldiers/poets in some hiding or temporary respite place, cold, wet, hungry, lonely, exhausted, terrified, and lice-infested, trying to make some sense or meaning from the ordeal, even if just to create a poem and find some comfort in words. Writing poems allows us to take off our "public mask" and express our deep-down true-blue selves.

I truly believe that humans, from ancient times to the present, are meaning-makers, and this contributes to our need to make some sense of the world, or at least to describe it accurately. It also contributes to peoples' need or desire to believe in a creator or a higher power of some sort, which also inspires some poetry. When life feels meaningless, as it sometimes does to people who suffer from depression, it can lead to despair. I have felt such despair on a few occasions in my own life, and would not wish it on anyone. Victor Frankly, a psychiatrist who endured a concentration camp for three years and lost several family members in the Holocaust,

believed that life had meaning even in that cruel environment. Helen Keller, one of my heroes, blind and deaf from the age of nineteen months, was also able to find some meaning in the darkest times of her life.

Many famous poets also had profound life experiences or struggled with depression and mental illness that fuelled their writing. Walt Whitman spent several years visiting hospitalized patients who had been wounded in the U.S. civil war, and struggled all his life to support himself. E.E.Cummings traveled to France to work as a volunteer ambulance driver during World War 1 and was interned in a prison camp on charges of espionage. Emily Dickinson lived much of her life as a recluse in her home, with few visitors. Langston Hughes was a black poet whose writing portrayed the real life struggles and strengths of black life in America from the 1920's to the 60's. Sadly, some poets like Anne Sexton and Sylvia Plath suffered from severe depressions that couldn't be resolved through their writing, and both committed suicide. One hopes that they found some measure of comfort or satisfaction in the writing of their poems while they were alive.

There is an art to reading poetry. It can be read silently, but it must be read aloud, even to oneself. Whether a poem rhymes or not, it usually has a rhythm that can be better appreciated when one reads it out loud. A poem should be read several times, and reflected upon. It doesn't need to be dissected, but savored, as one savors a delicious meal, letting the words, the meaning, the feeling, and the images be experienced as fully as possible. The great thing about poetry is that you don't need a lot of time- you can pick up a volume of poems and read one in a matter of minutes. Some poetry is

highly subjective and abstract- you can read it twenty times and still not understand what the author is writing about. I prefer poems that anyone can read and relate to in some way, or at least get a feeling from or a picture of.

The poems in this book are for everyone, especially those who are struggling with a crisis, problem, or important question in their lives. As a counselor, I have used some of the many situations that I have encountered in my work as subjects for the poems. Though many are written in the first person, they may not reflect my own personal experience, but a part of someone else's struggle. I hope that some of them speak to you.

On Being Human

It takes courage to grow up and become who you really are.   e.e. cummings

Fear

I wish my fear was like a stone,

That I could skip upon a lake,

Watch it bounce, then disappear,

Fling away this awful fear-

Oh, wouldn't that be great?

Shy

Please see past the plainness,

Please see past the fear,

Please see past the reticence,

Please just persevere!

Out of This Box

I wanna get out of this box I'm in,

This box of "how I should be,"

I wanna get out of this box of tin,

Rejoice in being me.

But only I can find my way out,

Away from these walls of "how I should be,"

By loving myself without a doubt,

No matter what others see.

One of a Kind

You are like a singular star in a thousand galaxies,

an intricate snowflake in a January blizzard,

a windswept pine in a vast wilderness.

You are like a speck of sand under a microscope,

a hidden marvel of shape, color, and design,

sculpted by the past, with a story all your own.

Never mind if the world sees plain brown sand:

will you be that glorious grain that is you?

- Did you know that every star in the solar system is unique?And that every grain of sand far more amazing than we realize? Look at Gary Greenberg's sand images at www.sandgrains.com

Grief

Some days it hits hard, like a fist in the gut,

and all you can do is drop to the ground,

crying out with a pain that seems

worse than death.

Other days it is gentler, like clouds that

gather and break ... gather and break.

As you feel them skimming back in above you,

you long for, but also fear the day

that they will be gone, leaving wide open sky

that you'd forgotten was such a gorgeous blue.

"If Only"

For such a useless, boring phrase,

It packs a lot of clout,

So very much depends on it-

And though it doesn't give a whit,

It fills one up with doubt.

It really has an attitude

For such a little runt-

That why it is so popular,

I'll never figure out.

The Breath

Silent but steadfast

it rallies on,

like the rising and setting

of the sun,

like the coming and going

of the tide,

like the waxing and waning

of the moon.

Isn't it strange

how we rarely notice

something so remarkable?

Here and Now

I wish we lived as long as rocks,
And had that span of time,
To try the things we dream about,
To iron all the wrinkles out,
And linger in our prime.

But all we have is here and now,
As long as it shall last,
To live as fully as we can,
Find comfort in our fellow man,
And freedom from the past.

You Belong

You don't have to be a tennis pro, or a movie star,
or an American Idol. You don't have to paint like a
Rembrandt, run like a gazelle, play the piano like Chopin,
or talk like a professor. You don't have to dazzle the world
with your beauty or talent, or hang your head because
you are plain. For you belong to this world, with its
endless variety. Is an oak tree better than a maple?
A hawk better than a finch? Is a rabbit better than a
groundhog, or a daisy better than a rose?
You belong to the world, with all your spots, bumps,
and wrinkles, your shape, color and size. You belong,
with all your foolishness, fears and regrets,
your worries and wounds and illnesses.
All you have to do is be who you are,
and offer what you can to the world.

Shame

Like a deadly gas slowly filling up a room,

poisoning its unsuspecting occupants,

shame fills the soul, leaving no space for joy.

The only exit is through the dark, endless

tunnel of addiction… pick your poison,

or stumbling and gasping through the door

of self-understanding, where you can breathe in

the fresh, clean air of forgiveness, and begin

again, with a soul that has room for joy.

Assumptions

Assumptions are like landmines-
mostly undetectable,
but loaded with destruction.

Comparisons

To stop myself from comparing
Is the trick that will end my despairing,
And though I know that it's true,
It's still awfully hard to do!

Regrets

I stand with my dog Molly beside the river's edge

in the quiet February cold, watching my regrets

float down the river, dip under the ice and back up again.

I watch until they disappear, little white bits of paper

that I have written on- seven of them, *seven BIG regrets.*

I know they aren't gone forever; they will return

in the night to keep me tossing, but I will lay still and breathe,

and imagine them again, floating down the icy current,

into the past, where they need to be. And as I watch the river,

I will remind myself of the dog that I am good to, the earth

that I cherish, and those that love me just the way I am.

The Big Picture

Look at the whole of the garden,

Not just the nettle and weeds,

Look at the medley of colors,

The flower pods plump with seeds.

Enjoy the warm, sunny yellows,

The deep cerulean blues,

The peaceful pinks and peaches,

And all of the purple hues.

See the whole tangle of garden

With its colors and textures and seeds,

For if you don't see the whole garden,

You may focus on troublesome weeds.

Wishing

I used to wish that I lived

beside the mountains

until I realized how spectacular

the clouds can be.

Oldster

Like an autumn leaf before it falls down,

Vibrant with color; red, orange, brown,

I am every age under the sun,

I am two, I am twelve, I am sixty-one.

I'm not just the oldster that young people see-

I'm fifteen, I'm thirty, I'm three.

On Being Strong

My mother tells me to be strong, but I don't know how. I have not survived a world war, or been ordered at gunpoint to leave my home, or wandered by wagon through cold strange lands as a refugee. I have not had to sail to a faraway place that did not really want me, or live with a stepfather who ogled my breasts but otherwise treated me like a nameless farmhand. I did not have to get married to escape from home, or live with a man who seemed to love his office and his whiskey far more than his marriage. I didn't lose my best friend and my sister long before they were ready to go, or open the front door to a stranger with divorce papers. I haven't lost parts of my body, not yet anyway, though I know that age will not pass me by. Oh, how I wish that she could lay her aching hands upon me, and give me some of her strength. But only I can find the place inside of me that is strong, even if it means reaching out for help. Only I …

Inner Critic

Y ou tell me that I'm homely,
You crow that I'm too fat,
You mutter that my hair today
Is horrible and flat.

You say that I am stupid,
You hiss that I'm a fake,
You target my incompetence,
and harp on my mistakes.

You seldom stop your chatter,
Your judgments never cease,
Inner Critic, go away-
So I can have some peace!

Change

Change can make you feel strange-
Upside down, a bit deranged,
Whether it's for good or bad,
Change can make you deeply sad.
But change can also make you grow,
Teach you things you wouldn't know
If your life went on the same-
Change is life, and life is change...

Anxiety Disorder

It runs in the family, she tells the doctor between sobs-
well, not sobs, but damn big tears that won't turn off,
like the gnawing in her gut, the fog in her brain,
and the terror that makes her so tight, she feels like she could
shatter into slivers of sharp glass on the cold tile floor.
Her grandmother, her mother, her aunts, they all had it,
had to fight it every day, with work and pills and words,
though it often answered back with meaner ones.
For years they fought, until they finally broke or learned
to stop the thoughts that fuelled it like gas on a flame.
She will keep fighting it too, with walks, and pills, and words
that she is learning to believe in, until at last it retreats,
and she can finally rest in knowing that she has won.

What Others Think

It doesn't matter what others think,

As long as I'm doing my best.

I don't have to act like someone else,

I don't have to pass a test.

So let people judge, surmise, and conclude,

They won't be able to ruin my mood,

As long as I'm doing my best.

Helen

She's ninety- three and almost blind,
She rarely leaves the house, confined
To audio-books, and tea with friends,
Telephone calls and plants to tend.
And though this woman can hardly see,
Her mind is more like fifty-three.

Despite the tremors she cannot control,
The fragile body that houses her soul,
She's happy to welcome each new day,
Even those that are cold and gray.
She loves a joke, her memories too,
I've rarely seen her feeling blue.

Though she's old and her body frail,

Though her heart has begun to fail,

She's not at all what strangers see…

I hope I age as gracefully.

Floating

Like a snorkeler, drifting

in the gently undulating ocean,

amidst graceful, darting fish

that glide with the waves,

I will surround myself with positive

thoughts, words and deeds…

but most of all, I will learn how to float.

Step by Step

A book is written one page at a time,
A mountaintop reached from a gradual climb.
So why do we live with such hurry and haste?
Life is a hike, not a race.

Envy

Like a parasite under the skin
tiny, but tenacious,
it gets more greedy as it grows.
Hard to get rid of, it can only be cured
with daily doses of gratitude.

Imprisoned

We've all been held captive,

some of us for months and years,

and others for a lifetime.

Not in a dark, narrow cell

made of dirty concrete blocks,

but a prison of our own design,

sometimes more formidable

than sturdy walls of stone.

Whatever it is that holds you

hostage, don't give up...

Keep looking for the keys

that will let you out.

 **Waiting**

My granny told me many times that
Good things come to those who wait,
I never quite believed her words, for
Waiting is something I really hate:
Waiting in lines when you're out in the cold,
Waiting for news you don't want to be told,
Waiting to heal, waiting to feel,
Waiting to make an appeal.
Waiting to die when you're ready to go,
Waiting for joy when you're feeling low,
Waiting for spring, for marshes to sing
Waiting to pack and take wing.
But the hardest of all of the waiting we do,
Is waiting for hope to fill us anew…
The darkness will end, just give it some time-
The light will break through and shine.

Linocut

Carefully I carve out the bits that

aren't needed, and my picture begins to take shape.

It can be a long, laborious process, but also

wonderfully surprising, like the carving away

of myself over days and years to become the person

I want to be, that only I can be, if I dare to embrace

both the black and the white.

Eyes

They
smile, scold,
laugh, love,
tease, trust,
probe, praise,
forgive, fear,
dare, dream,
beckon, beseech,
question.
How can
we take
such blinking
beauties for
granted?

Blind Woman's Wash

Back from the town laundromat,
she hangs the sheets and towels
and rags that were once her clothes
on the line between two tall pines.
She bends down and feels for the
bucket of clothes pegs beside her.
When the line is full she closes her
eyes and sees the flowered sheets-
the roses, pink on white,
flapping in the warm April breeze.
She breathes in the smell of earth, sap,
and soap; a smell that lives inside her,
and stands with her face to the sun.

Middle Age

Now that I've reached middle age

I hope I'll come to know,

Which dreams of mine to keep

And which I can let go.

Death

Death comes to all,

Be it early or late,

Dramatic or small,

Death comes to all.

Like a steep waterfall

Or a spring, more sedate,

Death comes to all,

Be it early or late.

The Other Side

I wish I'd meet a real ghost,

One I'd recognize,

A sympathetic spirit

On leave from Paradise.

I'd love to hear from Auntie,

To get the scoop from Dad,

And have some reassurance

That death is not so sad.

I'd like to know how Grandma is,

If Nan is somewhere near,

Though I hardly knew them

When they were living here.

I hope I have another chance

To see them all anew,

I hope there is another side,

Where spirits rendezvous.

Ninety-three

Old age isn't easy, dear-
I never thought I'd be
So worn and woolly-minded,
Though I am past ninety-three.

Or is it ninety-two?
Dang, I can't recall-
Never thought I'd ever get
To be this age at all.

My fingers, they won't work-
They're stiff as dried old glue,
They've got no strength or feeling;
Buttons I can't do.

My face is red and patchy-

It used to be so clear,

And if my eyes shrink anymore,

they might just disappear.

My hair now ain't much better,

It's thinning by the day,

Most days I keep it hidden

Underneath my blue beret.

My hearing aid keeps whistling,

My walker's in the rain,

My magnifier's disappeared,

Thank heavens for my cane.

Despite the pains of getting old,

I'm glad that I'm still here-

This nursing home my world now,

This lounge my far frontier.

But small things are enough today,
My room a friendly space.
I cherish favorite memories,
Those days of love and grace.

A cup of tea with visitors,
Someone's arm to hold,
A child's curiosity,
Questions, big and bold.

Death no longer frightens me
This knowledge I can bear-
That death and life are twined
Like the braids I used to wear.

I've had to let things go,
I've had to let life be,
But that is not so terrible
When you are ninety-three.

Words

Words are like violets blooming in spring,

A bright burst of color, a beautiful hue,

Like breezes in summer, they make the air ring

With a medley of sounds, familiar and new.

Some words are fragrant, like freshly baked bread,

And comfort us more than a favorite tea,

But words can also fill one with dread,

As deep and as cold as the open sea.

Words, like a bellows, can quickly inflame,

Or instead suck the life right out of a soul,

Be they empty of truth, or bloated with blame,

Words have the power to shape and control.

So... knowing how words can be more than unkind,

Oh, let me use words with love in mind.

Journey Within

I've started on a journey
To a place that's very near,
And though it may seem far away,
So fraught with dangers every day,
I'll not give in to fear.

I've got a good companion (me!),
Who will not disappear;
Together we will find the trail,
Through sun and rain and winter hail,
That leads from there to here.

I've started on this journey

To a place that's always near,

A tougher trek I've never known,

With sinking sands and walls of stone,

And caves where dragons jeer.

I'm going on this journey,

And I have to persevere,

I know that I can find my way

Through the land where dragons lay-

I'll not give in to fear.

THOUGH WE ARE CAPABLE of amazing things, being human means being limited; we will never escape from this fundamental truth. We were never meant to be perfect, but to learn to be better than we are now. Look around you at the natural world; life is all about being and growing. This includes "doing," but we need to remember that the *doing* comes from our being and not the other way around. Despite the limitations and imperfections that each of us struggle with, every human being is a miracle; a breathing, moving, thinking, feeling, imagining, creating, unique individual with the capacity to learn and to love.

I read a lot of Dr. Seuss books to my children when they were little, and my favorite is *Horton Hears A Who*. I admired that stubborn but humble elephant who wouldn't give up on his tiny invisible friend in *Whoville*. I always found the phrase "a person's a person, no matter how small" very comforting. Perhaps it was because I always struggled with feelings of inferiority. Just think of all the words that could be substituted for *small*! A person's a person no matter how *plain*, or how *smart*, how *large*, how *old*, how *slow*. If only this could be a worldwide mantra. There are limits, however. Is a person a person, no matter how cruel? If someone has no conscience, or feels no remorse, I'm not sure that they are human.

We all struggle with something; if we didn't we wouldn't be human. We all need compassion and encouragement at various time in our lives, especially if we didn't get much as children. No matter what we are wrestling with, whether it is an addiction, a mental illness, depression, anxiety, loneliness, grief over a loss, a health crisis or a traumatic event, we all came into this world as little miracles worthy of love and self-esteem. This wonderful core self often becomes buried in the muck of living in the world, like a pearly pink shell buried in the sand. We are beautiful not because we wear a certain style of clothing, or have a particular hairstyle or ability, but simply because we *are*, each one a miraculous living being, like the majestic buck with the big antlers that I spot now and then in the woods behind my house, standing still as a statue amidst a grove of pine trees. Some people spend their whole lives trying to get back this core self or sense of worthiness that was eroded or buried by negative early experiences. Our society hasn't made this an easy task, with its worship of youth, beauty, fashion, money, talent, fame, and so on. I have met many lonely seniors over the years, who feel useless and invisible because they cannot keep up with these expectations or definitions of success. After years of hard work and sacrifice, when seniors should be able to relax and enjoy the final stage of their lives, many feel that they are inadequate and have nothing important to contribute, especially if they have disabilities or a visual impairment that limits their activity. I will never forget the day that my elderly friend was transferred to the palliative care ward in the local hospital. There she was, sitting alone on her bed, fat tears rolling down her wrinkled cheeks, finally understanding that she would probably not be going back to live in her small apartment, surrounded by kind elderly neighbors. She had been active, busy, and upbeat until a few months ago, when her heart started to fail. Getting old is difficult without people treating you as if you just don't matter. I don't think there will ever be an excess of volunteers who visit lonely and isolated seniors.

It is not just the elderly that need understanding and validation- those with physical and/or cognitive disabilities and the mentally ill also struggle with negative labels and attitudes that make life difficult. We may ignore or minimize their complexity, strengths and creativity because all we see is the label, be it schizophrenic, bi-polar disorder, or whatever. A person's a person, no matter how they are labeled.

For many years I struggled with bouts of anxiety, and it is something I tend to feel ashamed of, even though some of it is likely genetic, as my mother, my aunt, and my grandmother all experienced periods of extreme anxiety. It is sad how much this sense of shame, of being defective and inadequate, erodes our self-esteem and contributes to both depression and anxiety. In many cases, we did not do anything to deserve the amount of shame that we struggle with, especially the victims of abuse and sexual trauma that sometimes live with pervasive self-hate brought on by another person's harmful behavior.

People with mental or physical challenges, who don't fit into mainstream society, and those in minority groups, are often compassionate and sensitive individuals; they know what it's like to be labeled, stared at, judged and treated with condescension; they are intimately acquainted with the damage that is caused by others' assumptions and ignorance. I know that I have become a better counselor because of my own experiences with depression and anxiety.

I am not trying to make heroes out of people with exceptional challenges, and I do not want to make excuses for people's behavior. There are consequences for hurtful actions, and times when we need to pass judgment on others, like when a friend of my husband's and his teenage daughter were killed by a drunk driver, who had a history of impaired driving violations. But there are many times when we need to

withhold the judgments and see the real person behind the appearance, the behaviors, and the label.

Many of us aren't able to love ourselves, which is just as important as loving others. We may have learned to compete and compare ourselves to others: that winning and being the best at something are what counts. As a result, some people are so afraid of failure or rejection that they find all kinds of excuses for not reaching out or taking risks, or trying anything new. But we don't have to be the best; all we need to do is enjoy what we do, to allow ourselves to simply explore and be curious.

Comparing ourselves to others often leads to powerful feelings of envy or jealousy, which eats away at us, as much as we try to hide it. Envy and jealousy can also lead to resentment and anger. All these feelings get in the way of happiness and contentment because we become so focused on what we don't have, or cannot do, and how we rate next to others. Such comparing is fruitless, like comparing a bird in the air to a fish in the ocean. Each of us has our own story, with its own unique beginning and subsequent plot. The wonderful thing is that we can enter that story any time and make changes to it, if we are determined enough. We are a product, but also the creator.

We have all heard about the importance of healthy self-esteem in order to cope with every day challenges, change, and life transitions. It is possible to develop self-esteem at any time, even after years of feeling inadequate and unworthy. The following is a "Reflection on Self-Esteem" that I wrote for the women in a support group that I was involved with, so they could post it somewhere to be read often.

Reflection on Self-Esteem:

In order to be at peace with others, I must be at peace with myself. This means accepting my past and present, my mistakes and successes, my strengths and weaknesses, my choices and behaviors. It means being open to knowing all of me. This does not mean that I stop trying to improve, or alternately, that I heap blame on myself, for many factors have contributed to who I am- heredity, my family upbringing, my school and work experiences, my relationships, stresses, losses, circumstances, and so on. Some of these things I had no control over. I came into this world as a valuable, lovable infant, as we all do, a child of the universe. What happened after that was not completely under my control, and perhaps resulted in feelings of shame and low self-esteem.

Despite all these things, I can find peace within, by taking responsibility for my own life, and by realizing that I can let go of past hurts that may interfere with my present feelings and relationships. I can let go of the anger that has built up over the years- anger at others and also at myself. I can forgive myself for my mistakes, and others for theirs. I can do this by talking to someone or by writing about it, or in other ways that work for me. None of us is perfect- everyone has a dark side. Our mistakes have an important teaching role in our lives. Did you ever stop to think what a perfect world would look like? No lessons, no learning, no challenges, no growth, no humility- in short, no humanity. We were only to become the best we can be, which will always be imperfect!

I can choose to love and care for myself, and enjoy my own company. I can choose to have more positive thoughts, to participate in activities that inspire me. I can choose to assert

myself in a healthy way with others- to say how I feel and what I need without becoming defensive or angry. I can choose peaceful thoughts over fearful ones.

It doesn't matter how I look or how old I am, how much money I earn, the amount of education I have, or what has happened in my past. These things do not have to control me for the rest of my life. We all have different starting places, abilities, and obstacles to overcome. I may have a steeper path to climb than some others, for reasons I will never know. I am part of nature, part of God or a Higher Power, part of this mysterious universe, and by accepting all of me, the light and the dark, and the same in others, I can come to find wholeness and peace within.

When my perfectionist voice starts jabbering away at me, I try to remember that we were meant to be imperfect, so that we could learn and grow. When I start a painting or a pastel drawing, I often feel discouraged with the initial product, because it looks so imperfect and amateur. I have to remind myself that beautiful works of art always start out that way. As I spend more time on it, thinking about colors, perspective, atmosphere, etc., it evolves into a real piece of art work, one that is still imperfect, but worthy of admiration. When I write a poem, it may start out as a fairly ordinary thought or a few unexceptional words, but over time it may evolve into a powerful image that someone may find inspiring. So too, we evolve over time, as we work away on the parts of ourselves that need improving. It is much harder to work on ourselves than a painting, for we continually have setbacks, and have to

begin over again. It often takes a lifetime to get to where we'd like to be, and even then we still have our flaws, the ones that resist change! As fallible human beings we are always in process. When we get discouraged we need to remember that there is wholeness in imperfection, because everything must have an opposite in order to exist. To understand light, there must be darkness, to understand joy, there must be sadness. There is a balance and wholeness in these opposites, though we can always strive for more light and more joy.

One of the best ways to be encouraged is to encourage others. By reaching out and giving, we receive that great feeling of being useful and contributing something to our world. There is always a need for volunteers out in the community, and boundless opportunities to give. One doesn't have to build schools in Africa to be useful; there are all kinds of needs close to home. If your self-esteem is low, volunteering can help it to blossom and grow.

Joining a group is another way to be encouraged, especially if you are an introvert or feel isolated. There are all kinds of support and interest groups out there- making that first step to join is the biggest hurdle. It is encouraging to find out how many others struggle with the same issues, long for the same things, want to be more connected with others.

Indeed, we have so much more in common than we realize, even though we may speak different languages and have different traditions. I'll never forget the most recent migrant worker dinner that our small church hosted to say farewell to the men who were leaving the surrounding farms to go home to their native Mexico and Jamaica. The organizers of the dinner had arranged for a steel drum duo to play some island

music for the men after dinner. After the first few songs, all but the shyest of the men were up dancing in the isles of the sanctuary. We were all dancing, Mexicans, Jamaicans, Canadians, black, brown, and white, enjoying the beat of the music, the men enjoying the freedom of a night out. I had never seen the church that hopping!

There is so much we don't understand about being human. Why do some people turn out so well in spite of a tragic childhood, and others become cruel? Why can some people cope with a scary situation, and others fall apart? Whatever our questions, we cannot deny the importance and power of things that are invisible, things that we cannot grasp in our hands, like love. When people are at the end of their lives, what is it that they remember most and still want more than anything? Love and kindness from others, whether it be family, friends, or even strangers that come into their lives. The feeling that comes from knowing one is loved and valued, and that one has also loved back. As I work on this book, I have been visiting a ninety-four year old woman who is in the hospital with congestive heart failure, nearing the end of her days. All that is important to her now is time spent with loved ones- someone to sit with, to hold hands with, to talk and laugh and cry with. During the long days in her hospital bed, where she cannot read or watch television because of her blindness, it is the loving visits and telephone calls that keep her going. It certainly has not been the hospital food! As long as love is near, she is able to let go of her beloved apartment, her clothing and possessions, even some of her dignity, as she loses control of her body in different ways and becomes more frail. Though we may deny it, we are all fragile beings that need to be treated with care, even the most macho of men out there. We know from the things we hear about many movie

stars and famous people that nothing can take the place of genuine love and empathy- not wealth, ambition, looks, status, or a plethora of material goods. In our affluent North American society, we often lose sight of these truths amidst the abundance that we have.

Being human is hard- we are bombarded with expectations, temptations, information, choices, and images of success that most of us cannot live up to. No wonder we sometimes feel overwhelmed and inadequate, and try to medicate our emotional pain with substance use or other addictions. Being human also means that we must experience loss and death, though we often try to push death to the periphery of our awareness. Whether one believes in life after death or not, leaving the familiar world and our loved ones, at any age, is difficult. Even though we are all dying as we live, and the two are that intertwined, we insist on ignoring death as much as possible. What would happen if we thought about our own deaths, not in a horrible tragic way, but in a peaceful way, for five minutes every day? Might we gradually get used to the idea, so that death wouldn't be such a shock when it finally comes? There is a poem about death by Mary Elizabeth Frye (1932) that I especially like, suggesting that we continue on after we die, in a different and freer form, part of the greater cosmos.

"Do not stand at my grave and weep,

I am not there... I do not sleep.

I am the thousand winds that blow...

I am the diamond glints on snow

I am the sunlight on ripened grain...

I am the gentle autumn rain.

When you wake in the morning's hush,

I am the swift uplifting rush

Of gentle birds in circling flight...

I am the star that shines at night.

Do not stand at my grave and cry-

I am not there...I did not die..."

    One thing about death that I like to remember is how many people have gone before me. Many more have died than are alive today- that's a vast number that have gone through the transition of death. If they could do it, then so can I, and perhaps they are waiting to welcome me on the other side, people that I've loved and those that I've always wanted to meet. I'd especially like to meet Gabrielle Roy, one of my favorite authors, to tell her how much her eloquent writing has meant to me. Death puts a frame around our lives, and just as a frame around a picture enhances the image, death helps us to focus on our living.

    But even with death in the wings, being human can also be a joyful experience if we remember to be compassionate to ourselves and to others, and accept that there are things we

cannot control or change. How ironic is it that by giving up control we sometimes feel more in control? Creating a meaningful life and being grateful for this sense of meaning, amid all of life's uncertainty, is what leads to joy, no matter how old we are, what we look like, how much money we earn, or what our past experiences have been like.

On Being in the World

*Love the earth and sun and animals,
Despise riches, give alms to everyone that asks,
Stand up for the stupid and crazy,
Devote your income and labor to others...
And your very flesh shall be a great poem.*
~Walt Whitman

One

We are billions here, and yet we are one-
One people under the moon and the sun,
One in birth and one in death,
One in hope and one in breath,
Everyone different, but also the same,
A yen to be known and called by name,
The need to be loved, and to give away love,
To eat good food and to have enough,
To play and have fun when the work is done,
We are billions here, and yet we are one...

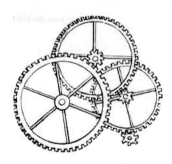

Differences

Imagine the world without borders,

Where people don't have to take sides,

A world without top and bottom,

Where people forget about pride.

Imagine us living as equals,

No longer consumed by hate,

Where people agree to be different-

Please tell me it's not too late.

Admiring a Basket

Who made this pretty basket that I admire in the isle
of this crowded, glaring store, full of odds and ends?
Was it a small girl, barefoot, in a bright yellow dress,
or a restless teenage boy, dreaming of someplace far away?
Was it a mother, worrying about what to make for dinner,
or a grandmother, remembering the stories of long ago?
And what about the hands that made it? Were they old and
rough, young and smooth? Were they brown or black?
Were they hands that loved their work, moving with an
easy rhythm, or were they tired of weaving baskets for people
in another world, people they would never see or know?
Did they work under a tree, gossiping with friends,
or in a factory, pushed and prodded by a cranky boss?
Suddenly the basket is not just another thing to buy in a
crowded store- I want to know about the hands that made it.
It matters, doesn't it?

Dilemma

I know there's someone starving
While I sit and sip my beer,
I know that homeless people
Sleep not very far from here.
I know that little children
Work much harder than they should,
While mine play hockey on the street,
So sure that life is good.
I know that I have far beyond
The things I really need,
And wish that I could sprout up
Like a hardy backyard weed,
In those needy places where
The hungry, homeless dwell,
With comfort food and medicines,
Enough to make them well.

I wish that it was in my power

To make the world more fair,

I wish that we weren't so afraid

Of what it means to share.

The Soldier

There is a statue in the park-

A soldier; solemn, spent.

Anguish in his eyes of gray

That time shall never ease; allay.

If he can know such agony,

This soldier made of stone;

Then what about the real men

Of mind and blood and bone?

Home From The War

He lies in the dark basement of his parents' house,
unable to face the day, to face himself without a leg.
The war wasn't worth his leg, he knows this without
a doubt. Though he slept better than usual, he dreamed
that he was running in a race around the bay, and he won.
When will these cruel dreams stop tormenting him?
He listens to a robin tap against the basement window,
as if to say *C'mon, get up, life must go on.* He listens
to the persistent *tap- tapping*, and for a brief moment,
he allows himself to feel a tiny flutter of hope.

Losing A Partner

Losing someone you love

Is the hardest thing to bear.

It hurts to be alone and

Face that empty chair.

The days seem a dream,

The nights drag on,

The world feels gray,

The joy all gone-

It's hard to continue alone

When you're used to being a pair.

Uncertainty

Uncertainty adores me,

It dances round me gleefully,

It wants to drive me crazy,

This horrible uncertainty.

As much as I despise it,

And wish it would be quiet,

Uncertainty will never quit,

Unless I make my peace with it.

Unrequited Love

I'm sorry that I could not love you

When you wanted me to.

Consumed with my own doubts,

fears, and voracious needs,

I could not be the person

you longed to be with.

Now, years later, I see you

in my dreams; I think of you,

and the love I wasn't ready to give.

On this quiet Sunday morning

I wish I could tell you

how much you meant to me.

First Child Gone

I still set the table for four,

forgetting you have gone away.

How could I overlook this, so quiet

is the house now, without

your constant humming,

your off-key crooning in the shower,

the dinner debates that

no one else could ever win,

the predictable requests: *Hey Pops,*

can I borrow your gas card?

Now we live on the edge of your

world instead of in the middle, but

I know that one day it will feel all right.

Making Pasta

She works in her basement kitchen,
sweating, and cracking eggs
into the soft, white, flour;
six eggs, to make a good dough.
Counting in her head the number of people
for dinner, reckoning how much
the grandchildren will eat, all those
beautiful, meatball-loving children.
What would her life be like without them?
She feeds the floury dough through
the press and spreads the noodles
on an old tablecloth to dry.
She thinks of the new batch of wine
they will serve at dinner, of the laughter
and the stories that will go on for hours,
everyone together around the table.

Love

Love is like a farmhouse light
In a dark and moonless night.
A beam upon an empty road,
A warming glow, a welcome sight.

Love is like a farmhouse light,
An open door, a kitchen bright.
A lovely lamp when one is lost
Inside a long and lonely night.

Wednesday Women's Group

You came every week in your wheelchair,
the only one in the group so limited.
And yet, you were powerful-
not strong or flexible in body, but your mind
so agile and active, a mind never still.
Every Wednesday, whether there was
wind or rain or slush, or you were in
one of those moods that sometimes gripped you-
sadness and fear of what may lie ahead-
you arrived at the door, ready to share your
stories, to listen to the others, who were not trapped
in a wheelchair, but paralyzed in other ways.
And when the group was over, you never
held it against them that they could walk
or even sprint to their cars, while you waited
for the special bus that would take you home.

I was glad that you were there those Wednesdays,

reminding me that if you could make it

through each day, then so could I.

Information Overload

I'm sick of information,

I'm tired of keeping up,

I'm overwhelmed with choices,

My head is full of stuff.

I cannot stand the clutter,

I'm bored by useless talk,

I need to find myself again,

I think I'll take a walk.

Town Square in Prague

I stand spellbound in this fairy tale world
of castles and bridges, arches and towers,
stone and spires that span a thousand years.
Each building unique, brimming with artistry
beyond compare; many lifetimes of hard labor.
What boundless ingenuity and devotion seeps
out of the carved stone and colored glass that
reign glorious in this enchanted place.

African Song

They voices merge into a sound

celestial, more vibrant than a breezy

hillside of tiny mountain flowers.

Voices that dip and rise

like waves upon a quiet sea,

or soar and plummet, like

the peak of Kilimanjaro.

Voices as gold as the grassland

awash in light; as ruby as the

setting of the Serengeti sun.

Nameless black children

beside a blank cement building,

filling the school-yard with a sound

that hints of heaven.

Billy in Hospital

I'll never forget that droll look; that
daredevil gleam in your blue-gray eyes
as you roamed the halls in your
oversized striped pajamas.
Freed from your infernal I.V. pole,
peering into rooms with that waggish grin,
you searched for a partner in crime-
someone to help you plant lizards
under the nurses' reports.

Munching on microwave popcorn,
the only food you cared to eat,
you prowled the floor for some action,
some new little kid to cheer up or
whatever else would chase away the fear that
sometimes crept up on you in Isolation.

Long after you got too tired for people

and pranks, I still think of you often-

your love of life, and your peace at death-

Billy, with the beautiful grin.

Serious

I'd like to be less serious-

It's just too deleterious.

I'd like to laugh and have more fun,

make each day count, one by one,

Like an otter in the water,

playful, carefree, curious!

Humility

God, grant us the humility
To learn from those we meet.
No matter what their circumstance;
The homeless, poor, elite.
No matter what their intellect,
Their schooling or their skill;
Leader of a company,
A worker in a mill.

For each man has a history,
His chronicle of time,
With all its complications, and
Discoveries sublime.
Lord, grant us the humility
To live without conceit;
To honor the humanity
In people that we meet.

Tell Me

Tell me what you feel,

But not with words that pierce,

Tell me what you need,

But please don't look so fierce,

Tell me what you're scared of,

I'll tell you my fears too,

Together we can tackle this,

Not let our anger brew.

At Home

It's fun to wander, fine to roam,

Good to end up back at home,

Where love makes up for scenery,

And trust for distant reverie…

Home.

Small Pleasures

In the hospital palliative care ward
three women volunteers came to sing,
and you, feeling rumpled and bored in bed,
and tired of smelling the fishy hospital lunch
that you couldn't eat, wanted to go hear them sing.
I came just in time to help you find your lipstick
and comb, and shuffle with you down the hall,
past helpless bodies slumped in wheelchairs.
Breathless from the walk, you collapsed in a chair
and closed your eyes, listening to the women sing;
their voices not perfect, but good enough
to let you imagine that you were at church again,
among old friends, and would soon be going home for a
grilled cheese and pickle sandwich, and a nip of brandy.

For that brief time you were not old or sick, or worried about your erratic and hammering heart, but only aware of small pleasures, like my arm hooked through yours, and three women singing on a sunny afternoon.

Dreary Days

Not every day can be a gem,

Singular and shining,

Some days are more like flat gray stones,

Unsuitable for mining.

But if there were no dreary days,

How would we recognize

Those wondrous, lovely, luminous days

Of azurite summer skies.

Happiness

We search for it relentlessly, in
malls and marketplaces, in gyms
and beauty salons and surgery rooms,
in mansions and yachts and shiny
convertibles, in fancy offices
and expansive boardrooms;
We look for it around the world,
in great cities, hot deserts, and snowy peaks,
in brothels and army barracks,
in liquor stores and casinos...
longing for the elusive secret of happiness.
Even when we don't find it,
we keep looking in the same old places,
forgetting that it will only be found
in a heart that is easily satisfied.

Slaves in A Rice Field

I can almost see them in the endless fields,
blood, sweat and dust congealed on their
dark skin as they work in the blistering heat,
longing for the cool shade of an oak tree
and the safety of their huts. I can almost see
the black muscled backs of the men as they
swing the gleaming sickles through the grass,
and the bright yellows and reds of the women's
head scarves as they bend over to collect it,
like flowers swaying in the breeze.
I can almost hear the rhythmic swish of the
cut rice, the low, melodic voices of the men
as they join in singing to pass the time, only six
more hours to go. I can almost hear the women
thinking, *please God , let Sunday come quickly,
the one day we can forget that we are not free,
Please God, let Sunday come.*

Imagine

Imagine the world if it could work

like one huge and never-ending

underground railway, but without

the need for a secret code,

the cover of moonless nights,

and cramped, airless spaces to hide in.

Imagine...

Remembering Joel

I remember well a

tall black Jamaican boy,

handsome and lean, a dreamer.

He was new to this country then,

without a father, or a brother,

living with a mother who worked

long hours to pay the rent.

He wondered why it was so hard to

fit in, to feel at ease here.

He wondered why he was failing

in school, even in art , which he loved,

and why he didn't really care.

Don't you want to graduate?

people asked him, looking stern. *You're*

older than the rest and still behind.

I want to be an artist, he thinks,

but his hands and his heart

are paralyzed with the fear of failing.

I want to be an actor, he thinks,

but I'm nothing special, thin and ugly,

so who will want me?

A year later I see him in the

grocery store, working in the deli.

He looks happy and at home, joking

with some girl- he was so afraid of girls!

I've graduated, he tells me, *and*

I'm applying to acting school.

We stand there smiling at each other, glad

to know that he has found his way home.

Gaza

My dog and I are the only two on this quiet meadow path flooded with sunlight, daisies, and fragrant purple clover. I watch the dog chase a butterfly, and think of people far from here, in Gaza, locked in their broken homes, with no food to eat, the air full of ash, and bombs raining down. As I listen to the fearless cry of a hawk above me, I imagine the anguished wail of a father who has lost his daughters, three of them killed in one blast, three girls with dreams, and the persistent hope that one day they would walk together, laughing, across peaceful sunlit fields.

Back in Time

Unplug the television,

Throw away the magazines,

Grant me some solitude,

Give me some nature scenes.

Bury the cell-phone, please,

Shut down the Internet.

Take me to a time and place

Where these things

Haven't happened yet.

Give me a sunny meadow,

Or the woods where trails wind,

Take me to a quiet place

Where I can rest my mind.

Eating Disorder

You could be *my* teenage daughter or son, with your scrawny arms and long toothpick legs, and the baggy clothes that you can't hide in anymore. You used to have a bum, your mother tells me, but it's disappeared. *All I see and feel are* bones, she says, *which are hard to hug.* Sharp and scary bones. Weakened bones that will easily shatter. *Where did we go wrong?* she wonders as we walk, fighting the urge to despair, thinking of you in the hospital. Will you get the help you need? Will you fight this enemy that badgers and bullies you? Can you learn to live with the fear that you try so hard to control? Can you learn to love yourself in this mixed-up world, where beauty means thin, though it's a such a lie; a hurtful, crazy lie. We continue our walk, and I see your mother's tears, or is the cold winter air that makes her eyes water?

I hope for her, but mostly for you, that you learn
to accept the uncertainty that is part of this world, and
believe in your own inherent beauty, which isn't dependant
at all on being thin, or anything else that people see.

Listening

If you think

that you have no gifts,

become a good listener.

For thoughtful, intent listening

is the ultimate gift, rare and precious

as a flower that opens in the night.

Work of Art

Make your life a work of art-

Grow your mind and know your heart,

Use your talents, be a friend,

Find a flower patch to tend.

Make your life a work of art-

It's never too late to start.

Ironies

What can you be tied to

that gives you freedom?

***

In giving up control, do we

sometimes not gain it?

***

In our living is not also

our dying?

***

Does not the potential for war,

the blood of millions, live inside

each individual heart?

***

Isn't being strong sometimes

admitting that we are weak?

***

SOMETIMES I FIND THE IDEA of being a hermit in the woods, removed from the world with all its demands and stresses, very appealing. However, I could only do it for a short period of time. After one or two weeks of solitude up north at a cottage, I am ready to rejoin civilization and relate to people again, and feel that I have some small impact on the world. Even Henry David Thoreau, the famous naturalist who lived alone in the woods for years, sometimes walked into town to hear the familiar sounds of humankind.

Like being human, being in the world isn't always easy. It is hard to pay attention to the immaterial things when we ourselves are material. It is hard to resist the temptation to satisfy our desires and the needs of our egos. Buddhism teaches that much of our suffering comes from becoming too attached to our desires and the things in our lives, things that we can never own because our time in this world is not permanent.

We like things to be orderly, concrete, fixed. We also prefer to be in control- we don't like the uncertainty of living in this unpredictable, often chaotic world. We want to put things in boxes with labels because then we have the illusion of control. We put ourselves, and others in boxes, and we even do it to God, whose presence we cannot even verify, never mind trying to describe God's nature.

It is also hard then to be authentic, to know the self deep-down, and follow one's own path, when the world wants us to be like Barbie and Ken. One of my favorite quotes on this subject is by Robert Louis Stevenson: *"To know what you prefer instead of humbly saying Amen to what the world tells you ought to prefer, is to have kept your soul alive."*

Society gives us messages, some blatant and others subtler, about how we're supposed to be. Attractive, intelligent, assertive, competent, independent, unselfish, social, interesting, happy, productive, well off financially, fashionable, worldly, and so on. Unless we have received exceptional parenting encouraging us to be our authentic selves and to value ourselves without conditions, many of us tend to feel inadequate when we fall short of our society's expectations. But who can truly meet them? At the very least, we are all sometimes incompetent, unhappy, and self-centred. Some of us were born with plain features or disabilities, situations beyond our control, and yet feel ashamed because we believe that we aren't attractive enough.

How do we live in the world and still be true to ourselves? I think by having one foot in the physical world, and one foot in the invisible, spiritual world. We do this through personal reflection, meditation, exposure to literature and the arts, giving to others, and spending time in nature. The more we practice these things, the more intuitive we become, in touch with who we are and what we want. We become able to see past the expectations and superficial nature of society into our own changing inner landscapes. We can question the world's definition of success and create our own. That is why some poor folks are more content than the rich; success isn't so much about personal achievement and recognition, but being part of a caring community.

Often we don't trust or listen to our own intuition, or we're so busy being in our boxes that we become confused about what we really want. Sometimes we believe that something will make us happy, only to find out that it makes us miserable. I have learned this through my own experience.

Several years ago, my paternal grandfather died and all the grandchildren received a twenty thousand dollar inheritance. I had really never known my grandfather as he had left my grandmother when my father was only four years old. Because I grew up without much contact with any of my grandparents, I would have preferred a close and loving relationship with my grandfather rather than the money I received after his death. However, I decided that I wanted to look for a piece of land up north with the inheritance- I had always dreamed about having a little cabin somewhere on the water. I think I was searching for a heaven on earth, as if that alone could make me a happy and complete person.

After choosing an area we could afford, we bought a piece of land on a small lake, alongside about twenty other cottages. I became so attached to that bit of land that I became obsessed with protecting it. I tried to control what others were doing around the lake, though this was futile because we cannot control others. When the noisy jet skis appeared, I began searching for something even more remote, using up the time that I could have spent relaxing, to look at other properties. I wasn't happy with this lovely little place we had found; I was miserable. I gradually came to understand that whenever we cling too much to things, whether it is land, the house we live in, the shape of our bodies, etc., we will ultimately be disappointed. We need to learn how to loosen our grip on things that we can never really possess, and I am continually learning to do that. We need to remember that there may be a fine line between passion and obsession. Henri-Frederick Amiel, a Swiss philosopher and poet, stated that: *"The fire which enlightens is the same fire which consumes."*

How do we stop living in a box? I think that we do it by realizing that we are not just what we think we are. We are part of something bigger, something we cannot get a hold of or explain. We are somehow connected to this vastness, this mystery, this universe and all that inhabits it. We have something in common with the leaves on a tree, the stars in the sky, the waves on the ocean, with each other, and with whatever began the whole process of life. When we become too attached to concrete things we lose sight of this bigger picture. We need to see the connectedness of everything instead of always thinking about our own little corners of the world. Why do innocent people die in wars that are waged by only an extreme few? Because we are not just isolated individuals- we are all connected, and so innocent people will die along with the guilty ones. When we ignore the inter-relatedness of all organisms, we make decisions that harm the environment and us within it.

From time to time it would be useful for us to remind ourselves that:

I am not my roles

I am not my self-image

I am not my past

I am not my illness

I am not my addictions or my habits

I am not my body or my face

I am not my feelings or my worries

I am not my mistakes or my problems

I am not my work

I am not my country

I am not my house or my possessions

I am not my relationships

All these things are part of our lives, but they are not who we are. My father identified so much with his work as company president that he was terrified of retirement, and kept putting it off. When he was sixty-seven, having decided that he would retire at sixty-eight, he found out that he had terminal cancer, with only a few months to live. Even then he couldn't let go of his job; he continued working from the hospital bed, until he was too sick to do any more. Despite the fact that he had a family, he had lived most of his life alone in that CEO box, and just when he started learning how to live outside it, sitting on his back yard patio, observing the birds and the gardens next door, which he never paid much attention to before, he died. The following year I went to Saskatchewan, where my father was born and had lived in a Catholic Children's Home because his mother couldn't afford to look after her four children, to see if I could learn more about this man who had been my father. I could imagine him flying a kite on the prairie, catching gophers for their tails, and throwing spitballs behind the nuns' backs, but I never did really get to know much about him; what he loved and despised, what he thought about besides his work, what dreams he never achieved, what he wished he'd done differently in his life and his relationships. I wish that I had tried harder to

knock on the door of his box, to encourage him to express himself and experience more of the world outside of his work life.

Another way to get out of our boxes is by being creative and experimenting with different possibilities, whether in the arenas of arts and crafts, music, dancing, making speeches, knitting, gardening, writing, cycling, starting a business, running workshops, and so on. Though we often cling to our habits and routines, we can push our boundaries and open ourselves to being more creative, even if we aren't loaded with talent. It's not about the skill or the finished product but the creative process of expressing ourselves that allows us to be out of the box.

Somehow we need to figure out how to live our lives as though they are important, but at the same time realize that, relative to the vast size and age of the world, we are small and insignificant beings. Like many other parts of nature, we are short-lived and fragile. Living daily with this knowledge, embracing it instead of resisting or ignoring it, would help us to be reconciled to death, and set priorities that focus on really living, and being content with what we *really* need as opposed to what the world tells us we need.

In addition to becoming more comfortable with death, we also need to believe that pain and loss are important teachers. I believe that suffering is as necessary as our hope to end it is. Helen Keller said it well: *"Character cannot be developed in ease and quiet. Only through experience of trial and suffering can the soul be strengthened, ambition inspired, and success achieved."* I try to avoid clichés, but some are so apt. Like the iron that went into a blacksmith's fiery forge to be heated and

then shaped into a useful tool, we also are shaped and made stronger by our suffering, though I do think that some people can be permanently damaged by their suffering, like child soldiers who have been taught to torture and kill, or children who have been grossly neglected or abused, and these are the people that we need to find ways to help, that remind us of the consequences of the evil that can exist within humans.

Even animals suffer in order that they may grow into something better or promote new growth. Though I don't know how it feels for an animal to give birth, I imagine that there is some pain involved. Birds molt in order to shed old worn feathers for new healthy ones. This process is known to be somewhat uncomfortable and very taxing for the bird. Snakes too, shed their skin when they become too big for it, and this process takes a great deal of energy, and temporarily affects the snake's vision, which is uncomfortable. Who knows what the caterpillar endures when it changes into a butterfly, or how a salmon feels as it battles an upstream current for miles, ending up at its spawning site exhausted, scraped and battered?

Most suffering can be borne if love is also present. Love has the power to ease suffering, and so if each of us was to love as often as we can, however we can, especially those who are not particularly lovable, then we could ease much pain and suffering. As long as we, or those in power, keep choosing the path of anger and violence, we will keep on seeing people suffer and die needlessly. Choosing the right path means being able to communicate respectfully with others, no matter how different they may be, to willingly put aside communication that is judgmental and destructive. It means letting go of the need to be right and to win. In my counselling practice

I see this need played out all the time in marriages, where spouses are so focused on winning the argument that they can't hear what their partner is saying or the feelings behind the words. Humility is a very undervalued quality in today's competitive world.

As humans in this mysterious world, we must learn to live within many tensions- the tension between individuality and community, the material and the immaterial, control and uncertainty, faith and doubt, wanting and needing, action and surrender, suffering and peace, love and loss, and so on. It is a challenge to find a balance, and this is also part of our life journey, to live the best we can within these tensions that are also our teachers.

On Being and Faith

Faith is the bird that sings when the dawn is still dark.

~Rabindranath Tagore

Searching

Like a morning glory,
probing and searching
for something to hold onto,
so it may ramble and blossom
deep purple or blue,
we, too, search for meaning
in a reckless world.
Hold fast to whatever it may be,
or keep looking until you find it:
art, music, nature, God, people,
pets, stories; whatever helps you
to ramble and blossom and send
down roots in a shifting world.

Inventions

I don't know how computers work;

They make no sense to me.

Microchips and megabytes,

Gigahertz and download sites;

Strange as fantasy.

Cookies, termites, firewall;

Words I can't explain at all,

And things I cannot see.

How they do the jobs they do,

With a simple click or two,

Is double-dutch to me.

And though I'm not a partisan

Of one belief, I understand-

If men can make such complex things,

Then couldn't God make man?

Maybe

Maybe God is not a man
Somewhere up above the sky,
With flowing beard and draping robe,
Wondrous ears and x-ray eyes.

Maybe He is also She-
A vast, eternal mystery,
A form that can't be known or seen,
But felt through you and me.

Do fishes in the deep-down sea
Understand the world we know?
Can ants decode the strange events
Of life beyond their hill and home?

Does a babe inside the womb

Know his mother's shape or face?

Can he see the great big world

That waits outside his little space?

Maybe God is not a man

Somewhere up above the sky

Maybe God is near at hand...

A message that lives in you and I.

Hold On

Hold on for one more hour,
get through just one more day,
Befriend that real human urge
To kneel down and pray,
Even if you don't believe
That God exists today.

Get through another evening,
Hold on for one more day,
Soon you'll find it feels good
To close your eyes and pray,
Even when it seems
That God is very far away.

God Within

In an acorn there's an oak tree,
In a cloud, the misty sea,
In a word there is a landscape,
In a note, a symphony.

In an apple lives the planet,
In a second there's a year,
In a sigh there is a story,
In a stone, eternity.

In a brick there is a tower,
In a minnow lives a cod,
In a seed there is a woodland,
In ourselves a piece of God.

A Lament

Oh God, where are you? I cry
as I curl on the cold floor,
calling for help in my despair.
It doesn't come.
You are as remote as the deepest
hollow in the deepest part of the sea,
as unreal as a singing mermaid
or a water nymph, a naiad.
Has all my belief been wishful thinking,
an unfounded legacy of longing?

Where were you when my father
coughed his last breath of blood?
When my aunt became a skeleton
even before she died?
Where were you when she

called out in the night, *I'm so afraid.*
Where were you when a friend
and his little girl, were killed head-on
by a driver way too drunk to care?

Where were you when so many Jews
were separated, starved, and slaughtered?
Tutsis', Hutus', Serbs', Croations',
and millions more, their stories never told.
Where were you when boys in the trenches,
bewildered and alone, were begging for
their mothers and the place called home?

Are you there in the prisons, small cells
without windows, where hope dies
though the body lives?
Are you there in the tin-roof slums that
spread throughout the cities,
mile after filthy mile?

Are you there God, are you there?

Can I hope? I don't know...
And yet...something whispers from within
that there is more than sadness and pain.
What about those moments of wonder,
the joy and laughter between the tears?
What about the hands, mine,
that rub my father's legs with lavender oil
as he lay dying; a small act of love?

What about those times that my prayers
were answered and suddenly I grew
by leaps and bounds?
What about that something unseen
that moves among us, around us, within us-
that eternal energy; erupting, evoking,
flowering, flowing, pulsing, pushing,
breathing, beating, growing, giving, creating?

What about the love and kindness that connects us

to one another, the pulse that gives us life,

the sprouting of all sorts of seeds into being?

A universe of design, motion, and meaning-

You must be there God, unfathomable,

a mystery- I hope you're there God,

in me, around me; somewhere.

Oh God, I want to know- *are you there?*

Longing

As a tree is rooted in the earth,

and reaches out to the sun,

we are rooted in the world,

and our souls search for God.

Country Chapel

A chapel in the clearing stood,

Made from local stone and wood,

In that silent grassy place,

A little frame of sunlit space.

That simple venue moved me more

Than any cathedral could.

Beliefs

Does God really care about what we believe?

Do our questions and doubts really make him grieve?

Or is faith more about the way that we live,

Helping and loving and learning to give.

I don't think he needs our beliefs to be "right"

He just wants us to live in the Light.

Watching The Geese

I'll get to where I'm meant to go,
Though now I may not know the way.
I watch the geese above and know-
My heart will lead me day by day.

Though now I may not know the way,
I turn my face toward the sky.
My heart will lead me day by day-
I'll find the strength I need to fly.

I turn my face toward the sky,
And leave my failures in the dust.
I'll find the strength I need to fly-
Abandon discontent, and trust.

Walking down this lonely street

I watch the geese above and know-

That though I have not wings, but feet,

I'll get to where I'm meant to go.

Farewell Prayer for Migrant Workers

Thank you for your hard work in the hot summer sun,

for the glorious harvest that you are a part of;

the produce that feeds our people and helps us stay healthy.

Thank you for reminding us that we are not the only land,

the only color, the only language, and the only way of life,

and for sharing your traditions- please teach us more.

May God bless you on your journeys home to your loved ones,

and may God keep you all safe and in good health.

May you find comfort in times of sorrow and hardship

and joy in the small blessings of each new day.

Rowing and Other Passions

Find your little harbor,

Launch your one-man skiff,

Leave behind discouragement,

And feel your spirit lift.

Find that steady centre,

As you learn to scull,

Feel the graceful rhythm,

The oar-blades catch and pull.

Celebrate the journey

As you row away despair,

Take time to do what moves you,

And let this be your prayer.

WHEN I WAS ELEVEN YEARS OLD, I was in a grocery store and noticed some headlines on a newspaper that said in large bold letters **"GOD IS DEAD."** I remember standing there by the checkout, immobile and in shock, wondering who would run the universe and keep things in order. I could not fathom how people in the store could just go about their business, buying cereal and jello and hot chocolate, as if everything was the same with God being dead. When I got home, I rode my bike to the Lutheran church that I attended on my own, to see if the Pastor could tell me what was going on with God. The pastor wasn't in his office, and when I attended church on Sunday, everyone seemed normal. The pastor preached his long sermon ("longer than forty miles of dirt road," I once heard a visitor say), the trumpets still sent shivers up my spine, and the choir sounded as passionate as ever. I decided, without consulting anyone in case I was wrong, that the newspaper had made a drastic mistake. I continued to walk to the river and hike through nearby forests, talking to God along the way, needing to believe that there was something bigger than me looking after things, despite the chaos that sometimes reigned in my life.

Faith is not a static thing- at least mine hasn't been. There are days when the possibility of God seems as real as the purple coneflower in my garden, and other days when it seems as remote as the days of the dinosaurs. There are times when I feel as though my prayers are not useless, but more often I wonder if they are just hopeful words in an empty silence. I wonder if I am simply deluding myself. And yet...I always come back to the idea of God. Is it because I simply need something to hold onto, a crutch, some might say, or is it

because there is something within us that is connected to a greater power we have called God?

I don't believe any more that God is a punishing judge who demands perfection- that intimidating image I formed from my association with church as a child. Some nights I would wake up crying, afraid that I would go to hell for some remembered misdeed, like secretly scrounging in my mother's closet for my Christmas presents because I couldn't stand the waiting.

Now I believe that God cannot be this harsh judge, because if this higher power exists, it must be better than the best of humans. If we are capable of kindness, compassion, wisdom, and appreciation for the amazing diversity in the world, then won't God be much more so? Would God have allowed for the human brain if he didn't want us to use it? Would God have allowed for such diversity on the planet if he wanted us to be all the same, to think in the same way? Would God expect perfection in a world that needs opposites in order to give it meaning, like light and dark, right and wrong, grief and joy? This difficult duality, built into life, is an important part of our humanity. Without it we would have no choice.

What is the case for God? The Bible? Well, that may be a piece of it, though after studying theology for a few years, I believe that the Bible is an earnest human attempt to define and understand God, but is ultimately limited and incomplete, though parts of it may be complete. After all, is there a better description of love than the one in the New Testament? Still, as much as we try, we cannot grasp and explain the nature of God- it is beyond our minds and our language. I do believe that the Bible, as well as other spiritual or sacred writings in

the world, provides us with important truths and insights, through the use of stories and metaphors. Once we get past the literal reading of sacred stories and focus on their meanings, we can discover truths that apply to our own day and age. For example, do we honestly believe that Noah filled up a crude wooden boat with two of every kind of animal and sailed the seas with them? Or do we believe that the story of Noah's ark illustrates the importance of taking care of creation- the land, the animals, the people that are all part of it. The story also reminds us that there are consequences for not taking responsibility to care for each other. The ancient legends of native peoples are the same- do we really believe in a powerful man on a mountain called the Windmaker, or do we reflect on the message of the story, which contains truth? When we listen for meaning, these outlandish stories become something more.

Does nature make a case for God? For me it does, though evolution is rather inconvenient and irritating in this regard. But isn't there order and meaning in the process of evolution? Could God not be part of that process? Just as a computer cannot put itself together, how could the complex and interdependent systems on earth just happen? When you see the incredible design, beauty, and artistry in the natural world, it is hard not to believe in an Artist. Why do humans have such a need for meaning and order if we were not meant to have faith in something greater than ourselves? One of my favorite stories regarding faith comes from a medieval Jewish philosopher. This version of the story is taken from the book *Why Be Good?* by Byron L. Sherwin: *Once a skeptic, who was also a great poet, came to visit a certain rabbi, who was also a poet. All through dinner they debated the existence of god, but the skeptic remained unconvinced. After dinner the rabbi showed* the skeptic to the guest room. On the table next to the bed, the rabbi placed some paper, a quill, and a bottle of ink. He told the skeptic that if he woke up in the middle of the night and wanted to write, some paper, pen and ink were available. However, tired from the large dinner, the skeptic soon fell asleep. Soon afterward, the rabbi entered the room. On top of the pile of blank paper, the rabbi placed a new poem that he himself had written. He placed the quill across the manuscript of the poem, and he tilted the ink bottle so that some ink spilled onto the manuscript. Then he opened the window a little bit and left the room.

In the morning the skeptic arose refreshed from a good night's sleep. Seeing the poem on the table, he immediately read it, and was delighted, for it was a beautiful poem with deep meaning. Later that morning during breakfast, the skeptic thanked the rabbi for the poem, but the rabbi feigned ignorance. So the skeptic led the rabbi into the guest room and showed him the poem on the table. The ink bottle was still tilted and the window remained open.

"I did not write this poem," said the rabbi, "but it's clear what has happened here. While you slept, a wind came into the room, tilting the ink bottle and causing it to spill. The wind then moved the quill across this page to produce this poem."

"Things like this don't happen by chance," said the skeptic. "The poem has meaning and beauty, order and design. It expresses the will, creativity, and thought of its author."

"Then," said the rabbi, "if you cannot believe that a single poem can be composed by chance, how can you continue to believe that the entire universe came into being by chance? Don't you think that the beauty, order, and design of the uni

verse also indicates that the universe had an author, a creator whom we call God?"

Most of all, what about the unexpected moments and experiences of grace in our lives? Those things that happen when we most need them to, that turn our lives around, answer our prayers, or help us through a dark passage? Are they all just coincidence? Something tells me they are not, that there is more to these experiences than we understand, those certain uncanny events that came along just when I needed them and helped to save me from drowning in the darkness that had permeated my life at different times. And what about those moments of remarkable beauty, which fill us to overflowing and seem to transcend the everyday routines of our lives? I recall a recent afternoon with my elderly friend in the lounge of the continuing care ward, where we sat after a walk down the empty hallway. Helen was exhausted even after such a short walk, and I could tell she was feeling discouraged. After a few minutes of sitting, a young volunteer entered the room and sat at the piano. He began to play a beautiful classical melody, and the music filled the room. The afternoon October sunlight shone through the large windows, and shadows danced across the walls and the floor as he played. The trees outside were swaying in the wind, as though they were moving to the music, and all seemed well with the world, though we were in a hospital where people were dying. The music seemed to wrap around the ill and the well, gently enfolding and connecting us, everything one. I could tell that Helen felt better because of this young man's music, and we returned to her room feeling renewed.

In the end, we can't really make a case for God, because we cannot prove that this "More" exists. Faith is a choice to

believe in something greater than ourselves, which we cannot see or comprehend. It is not an easy path in a world that reveres science and factual knowledge. Was Jesus truly divine, God manifest in human form to bring a message to the world? Or was he a profoundly spiritual person, who understood the nature and will of God better than anyone else? I don't have an answer to this question, but I do find that his words, his paradoxical, counter-cultural teachings, focused on love, forgiveness, and humility ring very true, and if they were acted upon by humankind, would transform the world. There is something special about a person with genuine humility, especially in a nation that prizes power, status, and wealth.

Referring to Jesus is not to negate other faiths or viewpoints. Why would God allow for such diversity if he wanted us all to believe the same things? Maybe he wants us to find the way to live together with our differences. Does it really matter what we call God, or what stories we use to explain him, if God represents love, goodness, compassion, forgiveness? These are things we can all connect to. Insisting that one way, such as Christianity, has a monopoly on truth and wisdom has caused all kinds of trouble in our world's history. Jesus was respectful of everyone he met, no matter his background or place in the world. When he challenged people, it was because of their hypocrisy, pride, or their judgmental attitudes, not their color, ethnicity, or particular faith group. We are united in our humanity, no matter what we look like, where we come from, what we believe, and how we name God.

When I first attended a seminary to study theology and counseling a few years ago, I was concerned that it would be too "religious", a repeat of the "fire and brimstone" version of

Christianity that I experienced as a child. It turned out, as things often do, that the seminary was a good place for me. It was not the rigid place I had imagined, but a caring place for fellow seekers to gather and share and debate and ponder, a place where I was able to express my doubts, and question things I didn't understand. It was not a homogenous group of Christian believers, but a diverse mix of people who wanted to go further than simply believing what they had been taught, who were searching for a faith that had room for doubts, questions, personal experience, and mystery. For example, one of the pressing questions I had was how much of our Christian doctrine actually comes from God. I've learned that much of Christian theology has been developed by man, from the time of the church fathers.

I also met many Christians of various denominations, who were flexible enough to consider different perspectives on Christianity. Some believed in Jesus as a savior, the Son of God, who died to forgive human sin, and others saw him as an exceptional spiritual teacher, a rabbi who did not plan to die the way he did, but was killed because of his radical views and support of the poor and marginalized. If we look to Jesus as the best example of how to live and what is important, does it really matter which perspective we support? When I think about the diversity in the world, the fact that there are thousands of different types of dragonflies, and that is just one tiny creature, does it make sense that God would demand us to all have and express our faith in the same way?

What I appreciated most about my time at the seminary was the fact that no one pretended to have all the answers, or even a lot of answers. I think that is one of the downfalls of organized religion in the world- we don't seem to welcome a

whole lot of questions, criticism, or individual thinking. We like to have our beliefs tied up in a neat, presentable package with clear guidelines instead of admitting that much of God is a mystery. Try as we might, we cannot pin God down like a butterfly on a board, and study him. I don't believe that there is one "right" set of beliefs. God is a mystery for a reason- it fuels our minds and spirits. What would the world be like if we had all the answers laid out? Marcus Borg, a modern day theologian and author of *The Heart of Christianity* writes:

"That Christian faith is about belief is a rather odd notion, when you think about it. It suggests that what God really cares about is the belief in our heads- as if believing the right things is what God is most looking for, as if having the correct beliefs is what will save us. And if you have incorrect beliefs, you may be in trouble. It's remarkable to think that God cares so much about beliefs. Moreover, when you think about it, faith as belief is relatively powerless. You can believe all the right things and still be in bondage. You can believe all the right things and still be miserable. You can believe all the right things and still be unchanged. Believing a set of claims to be true has very little transforming power...Instead faith is about the relationship of the self at its deepest level to God."

There is no doubt that religion has been very harmful to some people, particularly women and various minorities, but religion is not the same as God. As a feminist, how can I embrace a religious view that is so patriarchal, where God is consistently portrayed as a He? We must remember that institutionalized religion is man-made. And Jesus, though male, was not a macho sort of guy. He embraced the feminine in addition to the masculine; he expressed his feelings, he cried, he looked inside himself, he nurtured people, he stood

up for women who would otherwise have been abused or killed. He was a leader, but he led with humility. If we all were able to embrace the male/female aspects of ourselves, and see them as equal, would there even be a need for a feminist worldview?

To those people that have been harmed and cannot believe in a God, I would say; find your own path, your own way of connecting to or tapping into the *"the More"*- perhaps this means daily walks through the woods, time in a garden, volunteering with the homeless or underprivileged, fostering children, making music, working with food, painting pictures, writing poetry; whatever it may be.

The biggest challenge to my faith is the reality of suffering. Why would a loving God allow such terrible suffering to occur to innocent people? After years of reading on this subject I still don't have a good answer. The only thing I have come up with is that God's power can only work through you and I, since God wanted humans to have free will. If we didn't have this freedom, we would be like programmed computers or robots. Unfortunately, this power of the human will to make choices is one that we can misuse in the way we treat others. Because our freedom is an important part of being human, we must suffer the consequences of our actions or others' actions, and live with suffering. We cannot ignore our interdependence: the behavior of one person can affect millions of others. *We* need to be God's love in the world. We need to be his hands. This isn't easy, given our imperfections, weaknesses and stubborn egos, but it becomes more possible with the practice of opening ourselves to his words and living them out. How much suffering would be alleviated if we did this, and also if we each used our own suffering to reach out and

help others? There is no question that suffering develops compassion.

When my father was in the hospital after being diagnosed with terminal cancer, I contacted the hospital chaplain, not for my father but for me. I was in a state of shock and grief, especially because I felt like my father was still a stranger to me, a man who had loved his work more than anything else. The chaplain, sensing my fear of impending death and the struggle I was having with my faith, presented me with an image that I have never forgotten. It was the image of a baby in the womb, nearing the time of birth. The baby, though it does not know what a mother is, what she looks like or how she acts, senses her presence and her love. When faced with the birth canal, might this perilous journey after such a cozy, warm existence in the womb, not seem like death to the baby? It has no idea of what is waiting outside in the bigger world. If we apply this image to our lives, then perhaps death is not what we think it is, but a door to a different kind of existence, where we finally understand more about the universe. I can't say that that the analogy proves that God is there, beyond our awareness, but I like it. Richard Bach said something similar: *"What the caterpillar calls the end of the world, the master calls a butterfly."*

Faith may be a crutch, but if it is tempered with genuine humility, and the acknowledgement of the great mystery of God, it is a better crutch than many others in this world. Faith in alcohol and drugs, material wealth, appearance, status, sex, sometimes even human relationships, can be temporary, disappointing, and often destructive. Faith is like a farmhouse light on a dark country road, a beacon in a confusing and

complex world. A few of my favorite passages from the Bible are these ones:

"Love your neighbor as yourself. Love does no wrong to a neighbor: therefore, love is the fulfilling of the law." Romans 13:8.

"And if I have prophetic powers, and understand all mysteries and all knowledge, and if I have all faith, so as to remove mountains, but do not have love, I am nothing." 1 Corinthians 13:2.

"For where your treasure is, there your heart will be also." Matthew 6:21

"For what is a man profited, if he shall gain the whole world, and lose his own soul? Or what shall a man give in exchange for his soul?" Matthew 16:26

"What does the Lord require of you but to do justice, and to love kindness, and to walk humbly with your God?" Micah 6:8

There is a world of wisdom in these brief passages, a lifetime of guidance as we continually struggle to put them into action. These passages remind us about the importance and transforming impact of genuine love. We become removed from this truth when preoccupied with the material aspects of living in the world, but on our deathbeds what matters more than love? They also remind me that we can have everything- a magnificent home, money to spend, an extensive wardrobe, all the latest technology, and still be unhappy or discontented because we neglect our inner selves. The human ego is at odds with the soul and what it needs, and if we keep feeding our egos and fail to nourish the inner self, what have we really gained? Haven't most of us experienced

that feeling of emptiness after getting something we so badly wanted? The old King Midas story exemplifies this. One of the happiest times of my life was working at a summer camp for underprivileged children when I was a teenager: living out of a suitcase in a small cabin filled with needy, grubby ten-year-old girls, where I had no time to stare in the mirror, fuss with my hair, or go out shopping, no access to a car, a television, or even a hot shower, and the only entertainment was singing around the evening campfire, reading poems, and looking at the stars. That place, and the love I felt there fed my soul, and I didn't feel that I was missing out on something better.

Despite these truths I still sometimes wonder if faith is for the weak and naïve people of the world. But then I think of individuals like C.S.Lewis, a scholar, professor and prolific writer, known to be widely read, a brilliant conversationalist, and who endured his share of hardships. A determined atheist in his youth, he became a Christian in his thirties, and produced scholarly works about his faith. Lewis was not a weak or naïve person, and wrote openly about the grief and anger he experienced when his wife died of cancer, and yet he continued to believe in God. There are many others like him, who have not blindly accepted religion, but have examined it deeply and critically, and made the choice to have faith, however they envision God.

When it comes down to it, who am I to say whether or not God is real, and to try to convince others? I choose to have faith because I like having something to hold onto, something that gives some order to life. Though I cannot describe God with any precision or certainty, to me God is the deep-down knowingness of what is right and wrong. It is the inner voice

that nudges me towards compassion and wisdom and humility.

Someone else may have a vision of God that is quite different. It is when we put God in a particular box that we cause trouble in the world. If there is a God, I think that he is big enough to be called by different names, and to be described and appreciated in different ways. William James referred to God as "The More," and other names include *God, Spirit, the Sacred, Yahweh, the Tao, Allah, Brahman, Atman,* and others. Each of us has to decide for ourselves if there is a "More" or if what we see and experience in this material world is all there is.

If I had to sum up what religion should be, I would not talk about rules, doctrines or creeds, although these are comforting to some. Instead I would use this quote by the Dalai Lama: *"My religion is very simple. My religion is kindness."* The 19th century poet Ella Wheeler Wilcox said something similar:

"So many gods, so many creeds,

So many paths that wind and wind,

While just the art of being kind,

Is all this sad world needs."

Can it really be that simple? Jesus, too, stated that the most important thing about living a godly life was to love others. It sounds simple, but living it isn't so easy- there are so many

distractions, desires, and conflicts that get in the way of our giving. But yes, I believe that the essence of religion is kindness, and the source of kindness, of our humanity, ultimately, is God.

Mine may seem like a watered down faith, and perhaps it is. But this is all my mind will allow me right now. There are too many unanswered questions, contradictions, and ambiguities for me to be more assertive in my faith. To me, God is still very much a mystery, but a magnificent one, as shown to me by nature. Like Albert Einstein, *"I see a pattern, but my imagination cannot picture the maker of that pattern. I see a clock, but I cannot envision the clockmaker. The human mind is unable to conceive of the four dimensions, so how can it conceive of a God, before whom a thousand years and a thousand dimensions are as one?"*

Thus, I will continue to flounder about, loving, searching, praying, failing again and again, but holding onto the hope that I will eventually become the best I can be, with the example of Christ, and other wise and compassionate beings, to guide me.

On Being In Nature

Breathless, we flung us on a windy hill,
Laughed in the sun, and kissed the lovely grass.

~Rupert Brooke (World War 1 soldier/poet)

Landscape Inside Me

The lines in my skin are like ripples on a lake,

My freckles are like stars in the sky,

My curves and bumps are like valleys and hills,

My hairs are the grasses growing by.

My blood is a river winding on its way,

With tiny streams flowing head to toe,

My lungs are like the earth, swelling with the sun,

My heartbeat like the ocean's steady flow.

My thoughts are like the birds that flit among the woods,

My worries like a dark and swirling sea,

My tears are like the dewdrops that hang upon on a twig,

The land will always be a part of me.

Walking

My feet connect with the earth-
the mossy, pebbly, solid earth.
I sigh, and sigh again, deeply.
My limbs begin to loosen, and
my anxious mind unclenches,
like mounds of spring snow, melting.
My gait becomes a soothing song,
a hopeful prayer, a sacred beat,
as I pass through shards of sunlight
and a tangle of indigo shadows.
Woodpeckers warble, troubles dissipate,
and answers appear, like the delicate,
determined moths sailing across my path.
I stop and admire a pink spring beauty
peeking out from the dried brown leaves
and continue on my way, moving along
at a steady pace, but oh, so grounded.

Trees

Trees have taught me how to live,

How to bend and how to give.

How to reach for what I need,

To grow and thrive, at times

Concede to what life brings,

The ice and snow,

Storms and creeks that overflow,

Not resigned but rooted deep

Enough to sway in winds that blow.

Trees still teach me how to live,

How to bend and how to give-

Beautify my own small space

At my own uncertain pace...

Trees.

Winter Thaw

Snow falls from the trees

and glistens for a moment

in a shaft of sunlight.

All I hear is the tap dance

of a woodpecker,

a sudden surge of wind

among the boughs,

and the song of melting snow

in the pine forest.

Letting Go

Sometimes, like a river, we need to let go.

Relinquish that need to know and control,

Let go of the urge to please and appease,

To fix and to nix, to reach every goal.

Like a river that's flowing, fast and then slowing,

sliding and gliding, swirling and whirling,

Oh, what a joy to let go!

Just Be

Just be, like a tinkling brook,

Just be, like a steaming pot of tea.

Just be, like a blowing chinook,

Just be, like waves upon the sea.

Just be...

Sweet Technology

A feather might not look like much

But oh, what sweet technology!

So light and yet so powerful,

A strength you cannot feel or see.

A spider's web, a butterfly's wings,

Strength in all these fragile things!

Shades of Blue

A clear October sky,

A graceful dragonfly,

Shadows on the snow,

Some wild indigo,

A bold and bossy jay,

The windy Georgian Bay,

Let's see them all anew,

These lovely shades of blue.

A slice of berry pie,

An elder's twinkly eye,

A burning log aglow,

A distant mountain row,

A tangy concord grape,

A summer oceanscape,

Let's see them all anew,

These lovely shades of blue.

Swallows

Behind the school
The swallows' play,
They tease and tag,
A glad soiree.
They climb and dip,
They skitter and skip,
They kiss the ground
And soar away.

Night Sky

'Tis an awesome, incredible sight,
The night sky brimming with stars-
Those specks of infinite light,
Of which I am a part.

Loon

Fluttering, fluting,

Haunting, hooting…

Minstrel of the night.

Our lake Houdini,

Elusive genie,

You disappear from sight.

But please don't go away

For long; these hills

Are not the same,

Without you near,

Sweet sonneteer…

Bidding us goodnight.

March Morning

The drip and patter of the melting snow,
The gravelly squawk of an irate crow,
The steady plink-plunk of the maple sap-
Those singing tin buckets, and the scrabble and tap
Of a woodpecker, high in a dead oak tree,
And the cheerful twitter of a chickadee.
All these songs I welcome as I plod
Through the softening snow and the squelching sod.

The murmur of streams that will soon be dry,
The cries of flapping geese, favorite lullaby,
The sweet- water chorus tinkling through the air,
The flitting and whirring of wings everywhere.
All these songs I welcome as I plod
Through the waking woods, giving thanks to God.

In The Greenhouse

In your greenhouse lives a tree,

Reminding you of Sicily-

In the autumn bearing figs

As tender as a memory.

Through the winter, to and fro,

You carry water through the snow,

To keep alive the fruits of home-

The hills and lanes of Sicily.

While you work with rake and hoe

Do you think of long ago-

The days before you left to roam

A country far from Sicily?

Among your plants of Italy,
Your plum tomatoes, chickory,
You tie up every frail stalk-
Like a faded memory.

In your greenhouse lives a tree,
Reminding you of family,
On the farm that was your home,
In the hills of Sicily.

Diversity

So many different kinds of things,
Things with petals, things with wings,
Things down deep that leap and sing,
Oh, the joy variety brings!

The Meadow

This meadow is my thinking place,

An undulating, open space.

Where berries hide, all overgrown,

And grasses wave with simple grace.

I like to amble here alone

And theorize on things unknown.

Bid the trite to disappear,

Become the sky, a tree or stone.

My prayers are more wholehearted here,

In this lake of grass, austere.

Amid these daisies, eyes of Spring,

I do not feel any fear.

Secret kingdoms scout and sing,
Red-winged blackbirds trill, take wing.
A hawk sails upward, flashing white;
His cry, right now, is everything.

This meadow is my harbor light;
An earthy cove, a golden sight.
Where thoughts, like butterflies, take flight.
Where thoughts, like butterflies, take flight.

Tadpole in a Ditch

He swims through the icy melt-water
in the roadside ditch,
a tiny speck passing over the gravelly
bottom and the wet autumn leaves.
Oblivious to his tenuous future, he skims along,
finding joy in the moment,
in the simple motion of life.

Pine Tree

I look up high

on this cloudless day

at a deep green pine

in a sky more blue than words can say.

How I want

my life to be, myself to be,

this green,

this blue.

Starfish

They creep along the ocean floor
unaware of what they teach us,
not knowing that in the shape
of their bodies lies great wisdom.
Hold one up and you can see that
two arms point down to the earth,
that another two reach sideways
to the world, and the single arm points
heavenward, to the Something More.
If we can live out this lesson of the starfish,
grounded in nature, reaching out in love to
others, always remembering the
something more that sustains us,
we will learn what it means to be wise.

White-tailed Deer

Outline in the snow,
where you have curled up
beneath a young pine
as wispy as your tucked limbs.
A tangle of tracks where you
have browsed the sumacs and
leaped from the howl of coyotes.
I follow your footprints,
but the crunch of boots in the hush
will only chase you further away.
Though I hope for a glimpse
of your coat through the trees,
I am glad that you still
have places to hide and to rest,
gentle spirit of the snowy forest.

WE SO OFTEN FORGET that we are part of the diverse landscape that surrounds us and lives within us. We have internal peaks and valleys, dark caves and sunny meadows, barren desert places and vigorous, lush, forest. These internal places can be calm as a small lake in the early morning, or as turbulent as a tsunami, or anywhere in between. For many of us, our internal landscapes are uncharted, unexplored territory. We are too restless, too busy, too afraid, too ashamed to be still and experience them.

When I was a child I spent a lot of time on the banks of a nearby river, trying to launch various crude vessels into the current, to take me out to Lake Ontario. I never made it that far, but I had fun trying. It was as if the river sang in my own veins, allowing me to drift and ripple with it, instead of being the anxious and vigilant child I was at other times. The river was a constant presence I could count on. I didn't understand how it could keep flowing, day after day, year after year, never drying up. It was like the human heart, with a momentum of its own. When I was ten or eleven I discovered a grand bit of river that flowed a few miles from my home. I went there as often as I could, jumping on the rocks of the old dam, walking the riverside trail, crossing the shallow part with bare feet and jeans rolled up, trying to keep my balance on the slippery rocks in the fast-moving current. It wasn't a beautiful river, muddy and brown most of the time, but it was a place of wonder for me. I didn't understand how it could keep moving, never stopping, kind of like the human heart that keeps pumping for so many years.

If you have ever looked at a river from an airplane, it is a lovely sight, a shining ribbon that curves and winds its way through the land. Our lives are similar- we rarely travel in straight lines. We move forward, sideways, backwards and forward again. We make mistakes, bad choices, errors in judgment. We get carried away with our emotions, or don't listen to them enough. We have regrets that are hard to let go of. Yet, we can decide to let go, and slowly start to move forward again, into the present.

Because we have changing internal landscapes of our own, nature connects us to ourselves. Thankfully, nature is beyond the ever-growing world of plastic and man-made things, many of which we don't really need but consume us. Nature reminds us of the everyday miracles that we overlook; the miracle of seeds sprouting, the spinning of a spider's web, the migration of birds and butterflies, of amazing symmetry, mathematics, and design. And there is still so much that we still don't see in nature, things invisible to the human eye. For example, if you look at a feather under a microscope there are tiny hooks holding the barbs together that extend from the main branch. These barbules give the feather its remarkable but lightweight strength. If you examine a few grains of sand from a beach under a very powerful microscope, there is a whole world that we cannot see or fathom- each grain a different shape, color, and design. Grains of bee pollen also take on some breathtaking dimensions when magnified.

Nature also teaches us about the importance and beauty of diversity. On my own rural property are many different varieties of trees- ash, maple, beech, hawthorn, apple, elm, chokecherry, poplar, pine, spruce, and several more I cannot name. They all produce different seeds and fruits, which attract different kinds of birds and wildlife. In one square mile of land there can be so much diversity. In relation to different

races, cultures, and traditions, how can we possibly think that human diversity is a negative thing? That we should all be the same color, or have the same beliefs? Differences make the world so much richer and more interesting, though some people seem to find this threatening. I'm thinking especially of the places where women are still denied their individuality, where they are imprisoned behind a burka or veil. This "sameness" goes against the celebration of diversity, which is so much a part of nature.

Nature also teaches us that change is part of life, not something to be afraid of or avoided. Though life transitions can be stressful and sometimes overwhelming, they also encourage growth, new opportunities, and the development of character and strength. Symbols of change and transformation, death and rebirth surround us, but many are uncomfortable with these processes. I must admit that I'm not looking forward to aging, but resisting this normal change isn't going to be helpful. Sometimes, as hard as it is, we must learn to accept the way things are. Like water in a stream or river, we must learn to "go with the flow."

Of all the activities I do outside, walking is my favorite. So much can be solved by walking; my feet are the best medicine I know. When I am depressed or anxious, walking in the forest makes me feel so much better. It gets me out of the past and the future and into the present moment. As Soren Kierkegaard stated *"Above all, do not lose your desire to walk. Every day I walk myself into a state of wellbeing and walk away from every illness. I have walked myself into my best thoughts, and I know of no thought so burdensome that one cannot walk away from it."* Even the worst grief can be softened by walking because it opens us up

to see that we are all struggling and suffering together- we are all connected, to each other and all of creation, and death is an integral part of this life, even though we may not understand why.

   I will be forever grateful for the time I spent in nature as a child; glad that I did not grow up in the era of computers, video games and blackberries. Today we seem to have forgotten that nature will always trump man-made technology, as amazing and advanced as modern technology might be. No airplane can maneuver like a hummingbird or a dragonfly; no computer can mimic a human brain.

There are symbols and metaphors all around us in nature, just waiting to teach us something, if we pay attention. Ecosystems teach us about the importance of community and working together, the truth of our dependence on each other all around the world. Trees teach us how important it is to be rooted; grounded in some kind of faith or way of viewing and interacting with the world that gives us a sense of meaning and peace. Flowers teach us that blooming is possible, even under harsh conditions, and that small things can bring great joy. Meadows teach us the importance of being open and uncluttered in our lives. Fungi, so crucial in nature's ecosystems, teach us that appearances can be deceiving. Waterfalls teach us about the importance of learning to "let go" of whatever we need to relinquish control of. The lessons are never-ending, and have taught me more than any classroom or church, although I'm grateful for these places too. The divine, the human world, and the natural world are all woven together, although we have managed to separate them in many ways, to our detriment. Putting them back together is what will save us, and so...

"I thank you God for this most amazing day, for the leaping greenly spirits of trees, and for the blue dream of sky and for everything which is natural, which is infinite, which is yes."
~e.e. cummings.

An Old Celtic Blessing

May the blessing of light be upon you-

light without and light within.

May the blessed sunlight shine on you

and warm your heart

till it glows like a great peat fire.

Sandy Amodio is a professional counsellor and group facilitator in Milton, Ontario. She lives in a rural area of Milton with her husband, two sons, and dog Molly.

Her favorite quote in the world is this:

"We are each inside of us, a country with our own mountains and plateaus and chasms and storms and seas of tranquility, but like a Third World country we remain largely unexplored, and sometimes even impoverished, for want of a little investment."

-Dorothy Gilman

And her favorite verse:

"To see the world in a grain of sand

And heaven in a wildflower

Hold infinity in the palm of your hand

And eternity in an hour."

-William Blake